Making + MATH + Work

Whose Foot Is a Foot?

BY JOY VISTO

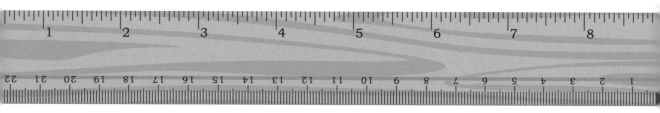

CREATIVE EDUCATION

CREATIVE PAPERBACKS

Published by Creative Education and Creative Paperbacks
P.O. Box 227, Mankato, Minnesota 56002
Creative Education and Creative Paperbacks
are imprints of The Creative Company
www.thecreativecompany.us

Design and production by Liddy Walseth
Art direction by Rita Marshall
Printed in the United States of America

Photographs by Corbis (Robyn Breen Shinn/cultura), Dreamstime (Rangizzz),
Getty Images (Howard George, Ursula Sander), iStockphoto (duncan1890,
HultonArchive, jeka1984, Meilun, N_design, OSTILL, PetrePlesea, Roberto A Sanchez,
Daniel Stein), Pixabay (OpenClips/18086 images, Preguntas Frecuentes),
Shutterstock (Laborant, Piotr Marcinski, Arkady Mazor, ostill, studioVin, Velniux),
Wikimedia Creative Commons (Pitke, Hugo Gerard Ströhl, Elly Waterman)
Vector illustrations by Donny Gettinger

Library of Congress Cataloging-in-Publication Data
Visto, Joy.
Whose foot is a foot? / Joy Visto.
p. cm. — (Making math work)
Includes bibliographical references and index.
Summary: A helpful guide for understanding the mathematical concepts and real-world ap-
plications of measurements, including classroom tips, common terms such as volume, and
exercises to encourage hands-on practice.
ISBN 978-1-60818-576-4 (hardcover)
ISBN 978-1-62832-177-7 (pbk)
1. Measurement—Juvenile literature. 2. Units of measurement—Juvenile literature. I. Title.

QC90.6.V57 2015
530.8'1—dc23   2014034840

CCSS: RI.5.1, 2, 3, 8; RI.6.1, 2, 3, 4, 5, 6, 7; RST.6-8.3, 4, 6, 7

First Edition HC 9 8 7 6 5 4 3 2 1
First Edition PBK 9 8 7 6 5 4 3 2 1

When you think about mathematics, you probably think about a class at school where you do **calculations** and answer word problems. But have you ever thought about math being all around you? It's in every shape and pattern you see. It's in every song you hear. It's in every game you play and any puzzle you solve! The first mathematicians realized this, and they looked for ways to prove it—to show how order and reason could explain much about life as they knew it. Sometimes this was easy to do. But other times, people just didn't get it. Even some of the most intelligent people in history have struggled with math: Albert Einstein once wrote to a child, "Do not worry about your difficulties in Mathematics. I can assure you mine are still greater."

So how can you use whatever you know about math in everyday life? When you find the *length* of your feet as you buy shoes, determine the *volume* of milk left in the gallon, or guess the *weight* of all the homework you have in your backpack, you are using math! Length, volume, and weight are the three basic measurements that are used in math. There are a variety of different **units** for these measurements, but the calculations you do with them have not changed. *Whose foot* was the one that helped set up the system we know today?

Prominent American

ALBERT EINSTEIN

Series

8c

MATHEMATICIAN – PHYSICIST
NOBEL PRIZE WINNER
1879 –1955

Artmaster

First Day of Issue

SO MANY MEASUREMENTS

LOOKING BACK ON ALL THE MATH YOU HAVE EVER DONE, WHEN DO YOU THINK YOU STARTED? The very first time you were involved in a calculation was likely right after your birth. Even though you can't remember it, it was important! One of the first things that happens after a baby is born is that their length and weight are taken. Such information is among the first facts that friends and family receive about a baby.

It's fitting that measurement is the first math that you were ex-

> WITHIN SIX MONTHS, A BABY TYPICALLY DOUBLES ITS BIRTH WEIGHT.

posed to, since mathematicians have been measuring quantities for hundreds of years. For example, when mathematicians first started doing math, they didn't understand numbers as being representations of quantities. If they wanted to talk about the number two, they would reference a stick or segment that was two units long. As a result, metrology, the study of measurement, has always been around and is closely related to all other branches of math.

The confusing part about using

units to stand for numbers was that mathematicians in different parts of the world had different names for their units. You probably have heard of units such as yards, meters, liters, and pounds. But do you know what a cubit, palastai, or digitus is? They may sound like strange words, but they are used for measuring the lengths of different objects.

A cubit was an Egyptian unit defined as the distance from the elbow to the fingertips. A palastai was a Greek measurement comparable to the size of a person's foot. A digitus was a Roman measurement equal to the width of a finger. Many other units for measuring volume or weight were also used in those ancient civilizations. Did you notice a common theme in how those lengths were defined?

If you recognized that the human body was the basis for the measurements, you would be correct! In fact, features of the human body have served as standards for units of length in civilizations the world over. Can you think of any problems that could result from measuring like that?

As Egyptians began building pyramids, they realized there were some problems with the cubit. They figured out that the "standard" was

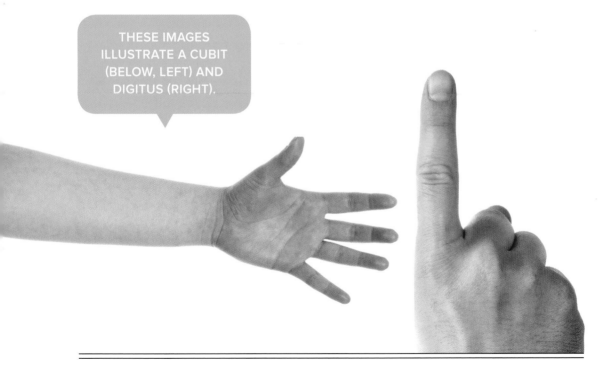

THESE IMAGES ILLUSTRATE A CUBIT (BELOW, LEFT) AND DIGITUS (RIGHT).

not so reliable, because the length of one person's arm might not necessarily match the length of another's. As a result, their cubits might vary. That would affect the execution of a construction plan—especially one involving as many pieces of precisely cut stone as a pyramid. So the Egyptians took a piece of granite and made a royal standard for the cubit. Then copies were made of that piece so that all measurements having to do with cubits would be the same.

Although body parts worked well enough for measuring smaller units, they weren't adequate when it came to distances. As civilizations traveled to new areas and attempted to capture the scale and scope of the world on maps, they needed ways of representing long distances. Measuring with the width of a finger wasn't going to work!

The Romans had a standard that they began using in the fourth century. They defined a length called a *pede*, which was very similar to our foot measurement. Five pedes were equal to 1 passus (a pace or stride), and there were 1,000 passuum in a mile. Essentially, the Roman mile was approximately 5,000 feet. That works out to be almost nine-tenths of a current American mile or one and a half times a kilometer.

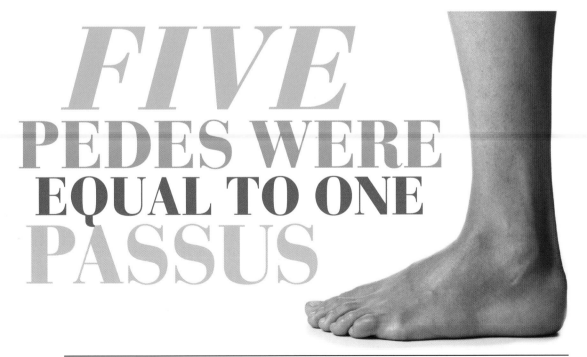

FIVE PEDES WERE EQUAL TO ONE PASSUS

IN THE 1800S, SHIPS NAVIGATED UNPREDICTABLY ICY WATERS TO EXPLORE POLAR REGIONS.

Measurements in the ancient world were particular to each civilization. There was no global standard in place. People spoke many different languages, and their units for length, volume, or weight thus also varied. As time passed, more and more units for measuring became standardized, thanks to the work of scientists in the 18th century.

During the French Revolution (1789–99), a **commission** from the French Academy of Sciences was formed with the intention of setting up a measurement system that would be used throughout France and in other countries as well. As a result, the metric system was born. The base unit for the metric system is the meter.

Just as the Egyptians had made a granite plank the physical "ruler" for a cubit, the French wanted to find a way to represent the meter. They decided to take a ten-millionth of the distance from the North Pole to the equator and define that unit as a meter. They even sent a team of people to measure the earth along a specific line of longitude and correctly calculate this distance! Over time, the meter has come to be defined as the distance light travels in a **vacuum** in 1/299,752,4585th of a second. The goal of that change was to create a standard that could be reproduced anywhere in the world.

After defining the meter, the group of scientists in the French commission worked to define the liter (for volume) and gram (for weight). Both of those measurements are based on the meter as well. For example, one kilogram is the amount of water that fits inside a box measuring one decimeter, or one-tenth of a meter, on each side. In fact, different units in

We don't have to convert A CUBIT, PALASTAI, or digitus!

the metric system can also be calculated by using **powers** of 10. Because we use a number system based on 10, this makes all the calculations done with the metric system easier. Those mathematicians were really thinking!

If you were coming up with your own system for measurement, how would you go about it? First, think about what your standard unit for length would be. A good place to start might be with the length of your own foot. You could even measure length by using pieces of paper as your standard. Do you think you would be able to convince your friends and family to use your new system? It wasn't easy for the founders of the metric system to get people everywhere to use theirs.

Over time, more nations have adopted the metric system, but not everyone has. In 1866, the United States Congress passed a law allowing the use of the metric system. In 1975, Congress passed another law to encourage optional conversion to the system, but no changes have taken place. In the U.S., most measurements use the English system instead. Units in that system include feet, gallons, and pounds. There is no common theme to how English units are broken down. For example, there are 12 inches in a foot but 3 feet in a yard. It lacks the simplicity of the metric system whose units are always in multiples of 10.

Students in the U.S. need to be familiar with both the metric system and the English system. Learning the basics for determining length or calculating volume is important because these skills are the same in both systems. As long as those skills are mastered, the task of learning how to convert, or change, between the two systems does not pose much of a problem. Fortunately, we don't have to convert a cubit, palastai, or digitus!

FIGURE IT OUT!

From Nose to Thumb

English King Henry I, who ruled around 1100, declared that one yard (36 inches) would be the distance from the tip of his nose to the tip of his thumb, when his arm was fully stretched out. This measure would set the standard for length in the English system, which is currently used in the U.S. If you measure from the tip of your nose to the tip of your thumb, how far is your "yard"?

SURROUNDING THE PERIMETER

SO WE ALREADY KNOW THAT LENGTH IS THE DISTANCE OF AN OBJECT FROM END TO END. Length can be calculated using any units. For example, sometimes people walk off distances to estimate how long something is. They are using their steps as units. However, the length of common objects is most often measured with a ruler.

Rulers have markings that designate different lengths with respect to the zero line. Those major markings usually count the distance in inches or centimeters.

There are smaller marks that divide the space between the large marks. Those divisions give us different **fractions** of an inch or centimeter. For centimeters, each little

INCHES OR CENTIMETERS

MILLIMETER, OR 1/10TH OF A CENTIMETER

mark is a millimeter, or ⅒th of a centimeter. For an inch, the middle mark (usually the next tallest), is half an inch. From there, the next tallest mark is ¼ inch or ¾ inch, depending on where it is located. Some rulers go down to ¹⁄₁₆th of an inch. In order to tell what fraction of an inch you are looking at, you need to count down to that mark.

To measure something, line up one end of it with the zero line. The zero line is the line on the far end of the ruler. It is not always the actual edge of the ruler! To find the length, read the ruler where the other end of the object stops. If the object lies between two lines, pick the one that is closer. Look at the following example.

In the picture, the segment (piece of a line) is halfway between the 9- and 10-inch marks, making it 9.5 inches long.

Now you try measuring the following segments:

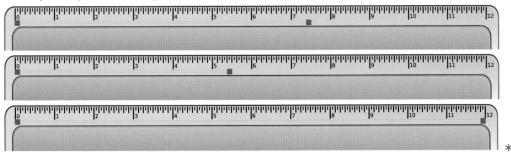

*Answer Key: Problem A

Did you know that even a broken ruler is capable of measuring things? Although you normally line up the edge of the object with the zero line, you can use any mark as your starting point. For example, imagine a broken ruler that starts at three inches. If you want to use that ruler, just line up your object with that inch line at three. Then read the measurement the ruler gives you. When finished, subtract three inches from the final reading. The segment shown below ends at eight inches, so eight minus three gives a length of five inches.

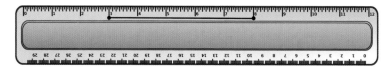

In doing this, you are essentially calculating length in the same way that you might find distance on a number line. If you have points on a number line, their values can be thought of as **coordinates**. To find the distance between two coordinates, just subtract one value from the other. If, for some reason, you get a negative number, take the absolute value of the answer. Absolute value, which is defined as a number's distance from zero, essentially just turns any value into the positive form by clearing away the negative symbol. Look at the example below.

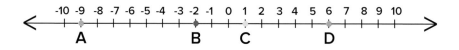

Find the distance between A and C, AC: A = -9, C = 1

A - C = -9 - 1 = -10

Taking the absolute value gives a length of 10.

Calculate the following lengths by using the positions of their endpoints from the number line above.

AB   **BD**   **CD** *

*Answer Key: Problem B

Mathematicians—and everyday people in general—measure length all the time. People buy their pants based on the length of their legs. In some track and field events, the winner is the person who has the longest jump. Perhaps your parents measure how tall you are on your birthday. There are many ways to use length.

Oftentimes, in class, the way you practice with length is by calculating the perimeter of a shape. Perimeter is the distance around the outside of a figure. If you know the length of each side, you can add them up to find the perimeter. For example, look at the shape below. What is its perimeter?

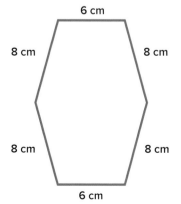

Adding up all the sides (6 + 8 + 8 + 6 + 8 + 8) gives a perimeter of 44 centimeters.

See if you can find the perimeter of the triangle and rectangle below.

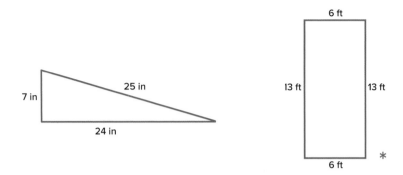

For the rectangle, you may have noticed that the opposite sides are identical; 2 are 6 feet and the others are 13 feet. This means you can use a **formula** to calculate the rectangle's perimeter: P = 2b + 2h, where *b* is the length of the base and *h* is the height. *P* is the final perimeter of the shape. You may have also seen this formula written as P = 2l + 2w. In this version, *l* is the length and *w* is the width of the sides of the rectangle. The two formulas work interchangeably—you can use either one to get the same result.

To see how this formula is used, check out the following steps:

P = 2b + 2h　　　**Always begin by writing the formula.**

P = 2(6) + 2(13)　**Substitute 6 for the base and 13 for the height.**

P = 12 + 26　　　**Order of operations: do multiplication first!**

P = 38　　　　　**Simplify and solve.**

The perimeter of the rectangle is 38 inches.

Is that what you calculated? Did you remember to include inches as the unit? Perimeter is always written in terms of a particular unit. Here, since the measurements of the sides of the rectangle were given in inches, your final answer must also be in inches. As you calculate the perimeters of the following rectangles using the formula from before, be sure to keep track of the units in your final answer.

Answer Key: Problem C

More than 2,000 years ago, Greek librarian Eratosthenes of Cyrene wanted to find the distance around the earth. He observed the position of the sun at two different places in Egypt. Then he measured the shadows created by the sun to determine the angle the cities made with the center of the earth. Using this information and the distance between the two cities, he calculated the earth's **circumference** to within 400 kilometers of its actual length!

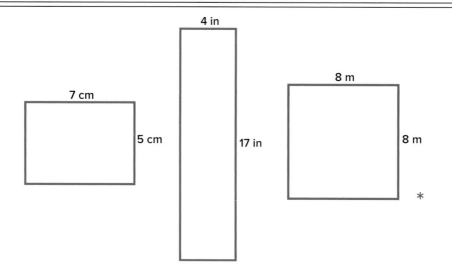

7 cm

5 cm

4 in

17 in

8 m

8 m

*

The lengths of the sides of a shape not only tell you the perimeter, but they can also help you calculate the area, or the amount of space inside a shape. Area represents the **two-dimensional** space of a shape. One way to calculate the area of a shape is to cover the shape in 1x1 squares. The total number of squares, each with an area of one, equals the area of the figure. However, most of the time, mathematicians will just use formulas to calculate the area.

The most basic of the area formulas is the one for a rectangle. The area of a rectangle can be calculated by multiplying the length of the base by the height: A = bh. Let's find the area of the rectangle (from page 18) whose perimeter we already know.

A = bh   **Start with the formula.**

A = (6)(13)   **Substitute 6 for the base and 13 for the height.**

A = 78   **Simplify.**

The area of the rectangle is 78 inches².

The units on an area problem are always squared because you are multiplying the units from the base (in inches) by the units on the height (also in inches). If you have trouble remembering which units to use, remember

Answer Key: Problem D

that area is the amount of space that a two-dimensional figure takes up. It may help you to think that the two from two-dimensional carries over into the units. Let's use the same rectangles whose perimeters you just found to practice calculating area.

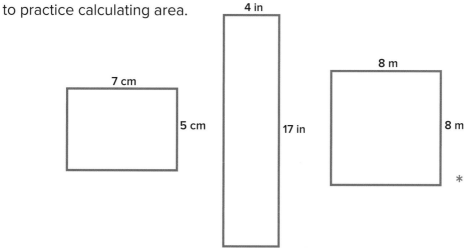

Another important formula to know for finding area is the one for a triangle. Picture a rectangle split from one corner to the other. You would get two triangles. The area of each of those triangles is half of the original rectangle's area. As a result, the area of a triangle can be found by taking half of the base multiplied by the height: $A = \frac{1}{2} bh$. The height must always meet the base at a 90-degree angle. Usually, this is shown with a little square in the corner where the two segments meet. Look at the following example.

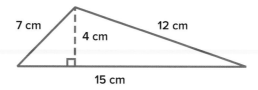

$A = \frac{1}{2} bh$	**Begin with the formula.**
$A = \frac{1}{2}(15)(4)$	**Substitute 15 for the base and 4 for the height.**
$A = 30$	**Simplify.**

The triangle's area is 30 centimeters².

Answer Key: Problem E

See how the height was determined by the segment that met the base at a right (90-degree) angle? The other two sides, with their lengths of 7 and 12, would be helpful to know for the perimeter, but they aren't necessary to find the area. As you solve the following problems, be careful as you substitute values for the base and height. Remember that the base and height meet at a right angle.

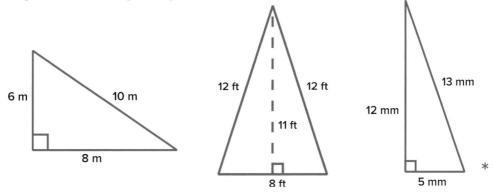

Once you've found the solutions, go back and make sure that all your answers have the correct units. Remember that the units on an answer for area will be raised to the second power, or squared. The units for perimeter will be written as normal. Area and perimeter are the basic measurements for two-dimensional shapes. But what happens when we add another dimension?

THE BASE
AND THE HEIGHT
MEET AT
RIGHT ANGLES

*Answer Key: Problem F

PAPER AND BATHTUBS

TAKE A LOOK AT THE PAGE YOU'RE READING RIGHT NOW IN THIS BOOK. YOU COULD DETERMINE ITS AREA BY FIRST MEASURING ITS BASE AND HEIGHT. However, this *book* is a three-dimensional object. You can no longer calculate the area. Instead, you will need to find the volume that the shape occupies in space.

Volume can be calculated based on an object's area. Picture 500 pieces of paper, stacked one on top of another. The area of one piece of 8.5 x 11 paper is 93.5 inches^2. Those 93.5 inches^2 don't change when you continue stacking more paper on top of the previous pieces, but the amount of space the stack takes up in the room does. The volume changes as the height changes.

Volume is measured in the same units as length, except it is raised to the third power to represent its three-dimensional nature. In the metric system, a liter is the standard unit for volume. A liter can be divided into milliliters and kiloliters. In the U.S., though, many other units are used. Perhaps the most basic is a fluid ounce. There are 8 fluid ounces in 1 cup and 16 cups in 1 gallon, which is also equal to 128 fluid ounces.

Another unit that is most commonly used is the teaspoon. There are three teaspoons in one tablespoon. But if you wanted to figure out how many teaspoons are in a gallon, you would have to know the following: there are 16 tablespoons in 1 cup, 2 cups in a pint, 2 pints in a quart, and 4 quarts in a gallon. It can make it difficult to convert between these different measurements when there are no common relationships (such as the metric system's usage of the powers of 10).

However, for most basic shapes that you will encounter in **geometry**, there are formulas that you can use for finding volume. When you work with such formulas, keep in mind that the unit used to represent the lengths of the sides will be the unit for the final answer. You won't need to worry about converting from cups to gallons or from gallons to teaspoons.

There are five basic shapes that you have may have learned about

TEASPOONS WOULD BE UNLIKELY TOOLS TO MEASURE VOLUMES OF SOLID SHAPES.

already: prisms, cylinders, pyramids, cones, and spheres. Prisms have the same **polygon** at the top and bottom (the bases), and all the sides are rectangles. Prisms are named according to the shape of their bases. For example, if those shapes are rectangles, the figure is a rectangular prism. Cylinders have circles as their bases, with a smooth side connecting the top and bottom. Pyramids have one base that is a polygon. The sides of a pyramid are all triangles that meet at the apex, or top. Pyramids, like prisms, are also named by the polygon at their base. A pyramid with a rectangle for the base is a rectangular pyramid. Cones are a lot like pyramids, but their one base is a circle. A smooth side, like that of a cylinder, wraps around the base and forms the point at the top. A sphere is essentially a ball. Mathematicians define a sphere as all points in space that are the same distance from a given point.

Mathematicians have a volume formula specific to each shape. The formulas for prisms and cylinders are very similar, just as the formulas for pyramids and cones are similar. For a prism or cylinder, volume is calculated with the equation V = Bh, where *B* is the area of the base and *h* is the height of the shape. In a pyramid or cone, V = ⅓ Bh. Because the bases for cylinders and cones are circles, their area can be calculated using the formula for the area of a circle, A = πr^2, where *r* is the **radius** of the base. For a sphere, the volume is calculated with V = 4/3 πr^3, where *r* is the radius of the sphere.

If you can calculate the area of the base, you have done most of the hard work required to find a shape's volume. Check out the following example.

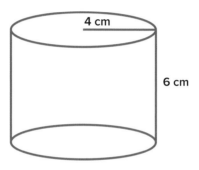

V = Bh   **Always start with the formula.**

V = πr^2h   **Because the base of a cylinder is a circle, use πr^2 for area.**

V = $\pi(4)^2$ (6)   **Substitute 4 for the radius and 6 for the height.**

V = 301.59   **Simplify by multiplying.**

The volume of the cylinder is 301.59 centimeters[3].

YOU CAN USE
either METHOD

In that problem, the formula for the area was substituted for *B*. However, you could just calculate the area of the base and then substitute that number for *B*, too. If that had been done here, the process would have looked like this.

V = Bh	**Always start with the formula.**
V = (50.27)(6)	**Substitute 50.27 for *B*, the area of the base, and 6 for the height.**
V = 301.62	**Simplify by multiplying.**

The volume of the cylinder is 301.62 centimeters^3.

As you can probably see, the answer is a little bit different because of the rounding that occurs when calculating the area of the base first. However, the difference in the two answers is very small. As a result, you can use either method for calculating volume as you try the following problems.

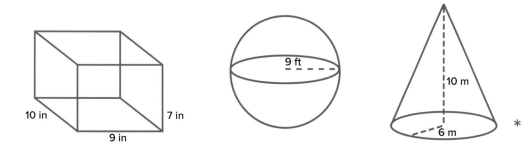

The volumes for these shapes are fairly easy to find because there are formulas that help with solving them. How would you calculate the volume of a more unusual object, though? When scientists encounter such situations, they calculate the volume using displacement. Displacement is the process that happens when an object is dropped in water and pushes the water up. In mathematics and other sciences, displacement is the method most often used for calculating the volume of many different shapes.

Answer Key: Problem G

Archimedes figured OUT HOW TO FIND *the volume of the crown.*

There is an interesting story about how this technique of measuring volume originated. It is said that Archimedes, a famous Greek mathematician, wanted to find the volume of a crown to determine how much gold was in it. He decided to take a bath as he was thinking about this problem. The bathtub was filled up to the top. When Archimedes got in, his body caused the water to overflow. As a result, Archimedes figured out how to find the volume of the crown.

What Archimedes realized was that his body needed space in the tub. He pushed out the same amount of water that his body took up. He could use a similar process with the crown. If Archimedes could sink the crown into a container of water, measuring how much spilled over the top, he would be able to calculate the volume of the crown, based on the difference. Look at the example to the right using tools called graduated cylinders.

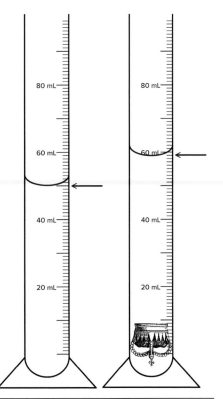

First, you need to know how much water is in the graduated cylinder. Whenever you are measuring the volume of water in a cylinder, find the little bowl-shaped figure that is level with the water. This is called the meniscus. Then look at the measurement that lines up with the bottom of the bowl. In this cylinder, there are 50 milliliters of water. After the crown is dropped in, the water level rises to 59 milliliters. Therefore, the crown has a volume of nine milliliters.

MEASURE
THE AMOUNT OF
SPACE TAKEN
UP

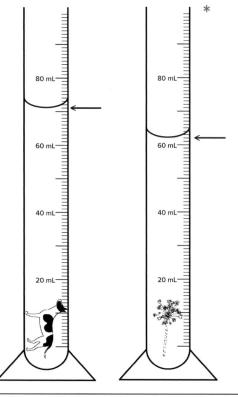

80 mL

60 mL

40 mL

20 mL

*

80 mL

60 mL

40 mL

20 mL

Can you use the same process to find the volume of the objects at left? To the far left is a dog, and on its right is a flower. Each graduated cylinder starts out with 50 milliliters.

In the examples shown, the volume was calculated quickly by using subtraction. So now you have two different ways to calculate volume—displacement and formulas. Between the two techniques, you can measure the amount of space taken up by almost any object you can imagine!

*Answer Key: Problem H

FIGURE IT OUT!

Platonic Solids

In addition to prisms, cylinders, pyramids, cones, and spheres, there is a group of three-dimensional figures named after the ancient Greek philosopher Plato. The Platonic solids are formed with regular polygons, shapes whose angles and sides are all the same measure. These five solids have special connections to the elements of the earth. The tetrahedron represents fire, the hexahedron (cube) represents earth, the octahedron symbolizes air, the dodecahedron symbolizes the universe, and the icosahedron represents water.

RECONCILING SYSTEMS

TWO FIGURES CAN HAVE THE SAME VOLUME BUT LOOK VERY DIFFERENT. Because of this, you may be more likely to describe an object by referring to its mass or weight instead. Mass is defined as how much matter, or physical substance, an object has. Weight is how hard **gravity** pulls on an object.

Because all the measuring you will ever do will probably happen on Earth, where gravity has the same effect all over, mass and weight can be used somewhat interchangeably. However, because the force of gravity is different from planet to planet, it is important to note that weight will change from planet to planet. Mass never changes, though.

Mass and weight are expressed in similar ways. The metric system measures mass using grams. Just as volume was defined with respect to length, mass is defined in terms of volume. A kilogram, which is 1,000 grams, is defined as

IT IS IMPORTANT TO ZERO OUT A SCALE BEFORE MEASURING OBJECTS.

the mass of one liter of water. (And a liter is the volume of a box that is one decimeter long on each side. The metric system always reverts to the meter somehow!)

In the U.S., a pound is used to measure weight, even though it is defined in terms of the kilogram. This definition of a kilogram equaling 2.2046 pounds was made official in 1893 with the Mendenhall Order. American physicist and meteorologist Thomas Corwin Mendenhall was in charge of a federal agency that mapped and charted the country. From his work, Mendenhall decided that the meter and kilogram should be the basis for the units of measurement used in the U.S. It's almost as though he was laying the ground-work for an eventual switch to the metric system.

The close relationship between the pound and the kilogram makes for some interesting conversations and mathematical analyses. It becomes possible to talk about how many kilo-grams are in 10 pounds, or how many pounds are in 10 kilograms.

Asking such questions involves making conversions from one sys-tem to another. These conversions are performed by using a mathe-matical technique known as dimen-sional analysis. It can be done between any two units that measure the same information. In order to change from one unit to another, you must know how the two units are related.

POUND & KILOGRAM

In the following example, you will calculate the number of kilograms in 10 pounds. You know from the Mendenhall Order that 1 kilogram equals 2.2046 pounds. You will multiply by a fraction equal to that relationship. That fraction is known as the conversion factor. Because those two values are equal, the fraction they make is equal to one. When you multiply by one, you don't change the value of any of the quantities; you just change how they are represented.

10 pounds × (1 kilogram)/(2.2046 pounds) = 4.54 kilograms

Notice how the units you are canceling are located in the **denominator**. Pounds appears in the **numerator** of the original weight and again in the denominator of the conversion factor, so those units will cancel. Just as 4/4 is equal to one, pounds/pounds simplifies to one, meaning that it has canceled out completely.

Using the same conversion factor, or the reciprocal, you can change each of the following from pounds to kilograms or vice versa. Remember that the reciprocal of a fraction flips the fraction over. The value of the denominator moves into the numerator, and the value in the numerator moves down into the denominator. The units travel with their numbers. Be careful as you set up that fraction for multiplying! The unit you want to cancel should be in the denominator.

14 pounds to kilograms   **4 kilograms to pounds**
120 kilograms to pounds *

What if, in that final example, the original weight had been measured in grams? There isn't a conversion factor that changes from grams to pounds. Fortunately, you could use dimensional analysis to convert between units within the same system, such as changing from grams to kilograms. The prefix *kilo-* means 1,000, telling us that there are 1,000 grams in 1 kilogram. After that, you could use another conversion factor to change from kilograms to pounds. Look at the example that follows,

Answer Key: Problem I

which changes 15,000 grams into its equivalent weight in pounds.

15,000 grams × (1 kilogram)/(1000 grams) × (2.2046 pounds)/(1 kilogram) = 33.069 pounds

You could also say there are 1,000 grams in every 2.2046 pounds. While the connection joining grams, kilograms, and pounds might be easy to spot when there are only two conversion factors with which to calculate, connecting other units will be more difficult as your conversions get longer and more complex. At that point, you should show the work it takes to do the conversion.

▶ FIGURE IT OUT! ◀

Light As a Feather?

Which weighs more—a pound of feathers or a pound of gold? This riddle may seem like a trick question, but the two quantities are measured using two different "pounds." Feathers are measured with the traditional system of weight, where 1 pound is equal to 16 ounces. However, gold and other precious metals are weighed according to troy pounds. A troy pound is only 12 ounces. That means the feathers are heavier!

When you write out all the conversion factors, it becomes easier to see which units will cancel out. Try the next three conversions. Carefully set up the fractions you are multiplying. To check your work, show the process of canceling units. If, somehow, you don't have a unit that shows up in both the numerator and denominator, then one of your fractions might be flipped the wrong way.

0.5 pounds into grams   **1,500 grams into pounds**

20 pounds into grams *

It's amazing how there can be so many grams in just 20 pounds! For this reason, mathematicians and scientists usually use kilograms when measuring mass. Kilograms give more reasonable numbers that are easier to talk about. Thanks to the math in dimensional analysis, it becomes possible to easily convert to kilograms or pounds, no matter what the units of the original measurement were.

Dimensional analysis works for units of any measured quantities. Below are some important relationships between different units of length and volume, many of which have been previously discussed. You can use them to do many other conversions.

Length: **12 inches = 1 foot**
3 feet = 1 yard
5,280 feet = 1 mile
100 centimeters = 1 meter
1,000 meters = 1 kilometer
2.54 centimeters = 1 inch
1 meter = 3.28 feet
1.609 kilometers = 1 mile

Answer Key: Problem J

Volume: 1 tablespoon = 0.5 ounces
1 cup = 16 tablespoons
1 pint = 2 cups
16 cups = 1 gallon
1,000 milliliters = 1 liter
1 liter = 4.23 cups
3.78 liters = 1 gallon
1 ounce = 29.5735 milliliters

Try the following dimensional analysis problems, using the chart to find the appropriate conversion factor. When you finish converting, see if your answer makes sense. One gallon is larger than one cup, so picture a gallon of milk compared with a cup of milk. It will take a lot of cups to equal 14 gallons. Your answer for cups should therefore be larger than the quantity of gallons that you started with.

123 kilometers to miles   **30,000 inches to miles**
10 inches to centimeters   **18 tablespoons to ounces**
14 gallons to cups   **16 liters to cups ***

As you worked through the conversions, you may have noticed that the process did not change, no matter if you were converting within one system or changing from one system to another. That's why dimensional analysis can be a helpful tool, especially as students such as yourself learn to measure length, volume, and weight for a variety of shapes and objects!

DIMENSIONAL
ANALYSIS *WORKS*

*Answer Key: Problem K

MATH TOOLKIT

1. You can think of the powers of 10 in the metric system as levels in a parking garage. The street level represents the main unit, meters. Going up 1 flight of stairs is like multiplying by 10 one time (dekameter), while going down 1 flight of stairs represents dividing by 10 (decimeter). At the top floor, *kilo-* represents multiplying by 10 three times, for a total of 1,000.

kilo-
hecto-
deka-
meter
deci-
centi-
milli-

2. In order to calculate area and volume for a variety of shapes, mathematicians rely on formulas. Formulas can seem overwhelming, with all the different letters and what they stand for. Keep this in mind, though: whenever you substitute a letter with a number, put parentheses around that number. It will help you track where the numbers came from as well as keep you from becoming confused as you start operating with them.

3. When you are working with formulas for calculating volume and feeling as though you are not getting the right answer, go back and check your work. If you're still stuck, go talk to your teacher. Be prepared to show all your work. Your teacher may not give you the right answer, but she will probably point you in the right direction. Teachers want to see you succeed. Don't be afraid to ask for their help!

4. When setting up a conversion factor, think of doing the dishes. Food scraps on dirty dishes are tossed into the garbage, often found under the sink. If you think of the units that you are trying to cancel as those scraps, they should go under the sink, or beneath the fraction bar. The clean dishes, the unit you are converting to, should go above the sink in the numerator. Converting is as easy as washing dishes!

GLOSSARY

calculations: operations performed on numbers

circumference: the distance around the outside of a circle

commission: a group of people who have a specific task to accomplish

coordinates: a group of numbers used to indicate location, usually on a graph

denominator: the bottom part of a fraction

formula: a rule that shows the relationship between various quantities

fractions: numbers that relate pieces of a whole quantity by division

geometry: a branch of mathematics that works with the properties of shapes

gravity: the force that pulls two objects to one another; on Earth, its acceleration is given as the quantity $g = -9.8 \text{ m/s}^2$; the value is negative because gravity pulls objects down

numerator: the top part of a fraction

polygon: a closed figure with straight sides that do not overlap

powers: numbers that have been raised to an exponent

radius: the distance from a given point, called the center, to the edge of the circle

two-dimensional: existing with only length and width, like a flat surface

units: quantities chosen as the standard for a particular form of measurement

vacuum: a space that is completely empty, including having no air

SELECTED BIBLIOGRAPHY

Berlinghoff, William P., and Fernando Q. Gouvêa. *Math through the Ages: A Gentle History for Teachers and Others.* Washington, D.C.: MAA Service Center, 2004.

Brown, Gary. "The Mendenhall Order." U.S. Metric Association. Accessed February 9, 2014. http://lamar.colostate.edu/~hillger/laws/mendenhall.html.

Dilke, O. A. W. *Mathematics and Measurement.* London: British Museum Press, 1987.

Lasky, Kathryn. *The Librarian Who Measured the Earth.* Boston: Little, Brown, 1994.

Rooney, Anne. *The Story of Mathematics.* London: Arcturus, 2008.

WEBSITES

Exploratorium: Your Weight on Other Worlds

http://www.exploratorium.edu/ronh/weight/

Find out what you would weigh—and why—on different planets.

Measure It!

http://www.funbrain.com/measure/

Practice measuring with a ruler with this fun measuring game.

ANSWER KEY

Problem A

This segment measures 7.5 inches.

This segment measures 5.5 inches.

This segment measures 12 inches, which is equal to 1 foot.

Problem B

The distance between A and B, AB:
A = -9, B = -2
A - B = -9 - -2 = -9 + 2 = -7
Taking the absolute value gives a length of 7.

The distance between C and D, CD:
C = 1, D = 6
C - D = 1 - 6 = -5
Taking the absolute value gives a length of 5.

The distance between B and D, BD:
B = -2, D = 6
B - D = -2 - 6 = -8
Taking the absolute value gives a length of 8.

Problem C

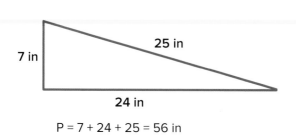

P = 7 + 24 + 25 = 56 in

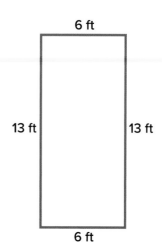

P = 6 + 13 + 6 + 13 = 38 ft

Problem D

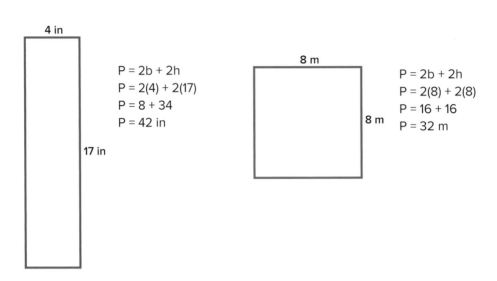

7 cm

5 cm

P = 2b + 2h
P = 2(7) + 2(5)
P = 14 + 10
P = 24 cm

4 in

17 in

P = 2b + 2h
P = 2(4) + 2(17)
P = 8 + 34
P = 42 in

8 m

8 m

P = 2b + 2h
P = 2(8) + 2(8)
P = 16 + 16
P = 32 m

Problem E

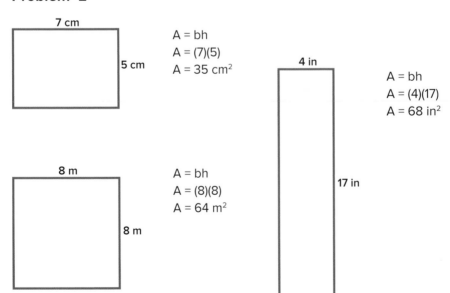

7 cm

5 cm

A = bh
A = (7)(5)
A = 35 cm^2

4 in

17 in

A = bh
A = (4)(17)
A = 68 in^2

8 m

8 m

A = bh
A = (8)(8)
A = 64 m^2

Problem F

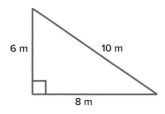

A = 1/2 bh
A = 1/2(8)(6)
A = 24 m²

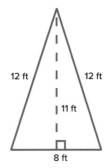

A = 1/2 bh
A = 1/2(8)(11)
A = 44 ft²

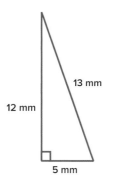

A = 1/2 bh
A = 1/2(5)(12)
A = 30 mm²

Problem G

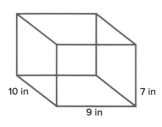

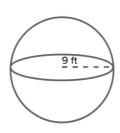

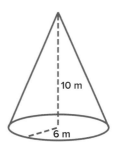

V = Bh
B = bh = (10)(9) = 90
V = (90)(7)
V = 630 in³

V = 4/3 πr³
V = 4/3 π(9)³
V = 3,053.63 ft³

V = 1/3 Bh
B = πr² = π(6)²= 113.10
V = 1/3(113.10)(10)
V = 376.99 m³

Problem H

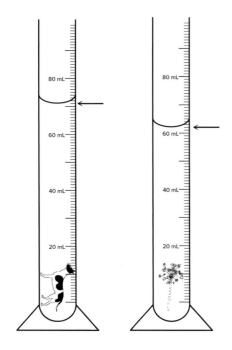

The final volume is 71 milliliters.
71 - 50 = 21.
The volume of the dog is 21 milliliters.

The final volume is 62 milliliters.
62 - 50 = 12
The volume of the flower is 12 milliliters.

Problem I

14 pounds to kilograms:
14 pounds × (1 kilogram)/(2.2046 pounds) = 6.35 kilograms
4 kilograms to pounds:
4 kilograms × (2.2046 pounds)/(1 kilogram) = 8.82 pounds
120 kilograms to pounds:
120 kilograms × (2.2046 pounds)/(1 kilogram) = 264.55 pounds

Problem J

0.5 pounds into grams: 0.5 pounds × (1 kilogram)/(2.2046 pounds) × (1000 grams)/(1 kilogram) = 226.80 grams
1,500 grams into pounds: 1,500 grams × (1 kilogram)/(1000 grams) × (2.2046 pounds)/(1 kilogram) = 3.31 pounds
20 pounds into grams: 20 pounds × (1 kilogram)/(2.2046 pounds) × (1000 grams)/(1 kilogram) = 9,071.94 grams

Problem K

123 kilometers to miles: 123 kilometers × (1 mile)/(1.609 kilometers) = 76.44 miles
30,000 inches to miles: 30,000 inches × (1 foot)/(12 inches) × (1 mile)/(5280 feet) = .47 miles
10 inches to centimeters: 10 inches × (2.54 centimeters)/(1 inch) = 25.4 centimeters
18 tablespoons to ounces: 18 tablespoons × (0.5 ounces)/(1 tablespoon) = 9 ounces
14 gallons to cups: 14 gallons × (16 cups)/(1 gallon) = 224 cups
16 liters to cups: 16 liters × (4.23 cups)/(1 liter) = 67.68 cups